SIMPLE COOKERY

Pasta

igloo

Published in 2011
by Igloo Books Ltd
Cottage Farm
Sywell
NN6 0BJ
www.igloo-books.com

2 4 6 8 10 9 7 5 3 1

ISBN: 978 0 85734 9 859

Project Managed by R&R Publications Marketing Pty Ltd

Food Photography: R&R Photostudio (www.rrphotostudio.com.au)
Recipe Development: R&R Test Kitchen

Printed in and manufactured in China

Contents

Cappellini with Tomatoes, Garlic and Basil

Prep and cook time: 45 minutes   Serves: 4

60 ml / 5 fl. oz / ¼ cup olive oil

6 cloves of garlic, thinly sliced

500g / 18oz tomatoes, diced

⅓ cup basil, shredded

salt and freshly ground black pepper

400g / 14oz cappellini

Heat the oil in a pan, add the garlic and cook over a medium heat until the garlic is slightly browned and golden.

Reduce the heat, add tomatoes, basil, salt and pepper, and cook for 5 minutes.

Bring a large saucepan of salted water to the boil, add the cappellini and cook for 8 minutes, or al dente. Drain.

Serve the cappellini with the tomato sauce.

Creamy Pasta with Leeks and Zucchini

Prep and cook time: 35 minutes   Serves: 4

275g / 9oz dried pasta bows or spirals

1 large leek, sliced

50g / 2oz frozen peas

4 tomatoes

25g / 1oz butter

1 clove of garlic, crushed

2 courgettes (zucchini), halved and sliced

200ml / 7 fl oz crème fraîche

1 tbsp tomato purée

2 tbsp chopped fresh basil

freshly ground black pepper

4 tbsps Parmesan, grated

Cook the pasta according to the packet instructions. When it is almost firm to the bite, add the leeks and peas and cook for 2 minutes, until the pasta is cooked and the vegetables have softened. Drain well.

Put the tomatoes in a bowl, cover with boiling water and leave for 30 seconds. Peel, deseed, then chop them and set aside. Heat the butter in a large skillet, then add the garlic and zucchini. Fry for 5 minutes, stirring frequently, until lightly golden.

Reduce the heat and stir in the crème fraîche and tomato purée. Add the chopped tomatoes, basil and seasoning and simmer for 5 minutes to heat through. Stir the pasta with the leeks and peas into the sauce and serve sprinkled with Parmesan.

Easy Mushroom Linguine

Prep and cook time: 40 minutess   Serves: 4

500g / 18oz mixed mushrooms

20g / 1oz butter

2 cloves of garlic, crushed

125ml / 4.5 fl.oz / ½ cup white wine

2 sprigs thyme, leaves chopped

1 tsp freshly ground black pepper

500g / 18oz linguine

Cook the mushrooms in the butter and crushed garlic, add the white wine, thyme and black pepper. Cook for a few minutes until combined.

Bring a large saucepan of salted water to the boil, add the pasta and cook for 8 minutes or until just firm in the center (al dente). Drain, divide among four serving bowls and top with the mushrooom mixture.

Fettuccine Nello

Prep and cook time: 25 minutes

Serves 4

500g / 18oz fresh fettuccine
1 tbsp salt
1 tbsp olive oil
1 red pepper, finely chopped
3 cloves of garlic, crushed
1 lemon, juice and zest
2 tbsps salted capers, rinsed
¼ cup flat leaf parsley, chopped
freshly ground black pepper
1 tbsp butter

Place the pasta of boiling water in a large saucepan with salt and cook for 8 minutes, or until al dente. Drain, set aside and keep warm.

To make the sauce, heat the oil in a saucepan over a medium heat, add the pepper and cook, stirring for 3 minutes. Add the garlic and zest and cook for a further 2 minutes. Add the capers, parsley and black pepper and cook for 2 minutes, then add the butter. Remove from the heat and add lemon juice. Spoon the sauce over pasta and combine well.

Fettuccine with Vegetables

Prep and cook time: 30 minutes　　Serves 4

2 fennel bulbs, stalks removed

450g / 1lb asparagus, trimmed

60 ml / 2 fl. oz extra-virgin olive oil

sea salt and freshly ground pepper

1 cup green peas

450g / 1lb fettuccine

2 tbsps flat-leaf parsley, chopped

1 tbsp rosemary, chopped

1 tbsp mint, chopped

1 lemon, zest

45g / 1.5 oz Parmesan cheese, grated

425g / 1lb canned cannellini beans, drained and rinsed

Cut fennel bulbs into coarse slices. Cut asparagus into pieces and combine with fennel in a bowl. Drizzle over 1 tablespoon of the oil and season with salt and pepper.

Grill until just tender. Return the warm vegetables to a bowl and add peas.

Cook the pasta in salted, boiling water according to package directions. Drain and pour into a large serving bowl.

Add the vegetables, the remainder of the oil, the parsley, rosemary, mint, lemon zest, cheese and cannellini beans, and season with more salt and pepper.

Chicken Rissoles in Tomato Sauce

Prep and cook time: 1 hour 10 minutes   Serves 4

500g / 18oz chicken, ground
1 medium onion
¼ cup parsley, finely chopped
½ tsp salt
black pepper
1 egg
½ cup breadcrumbs, dried
1 tbsp water
oil for frying

Tomato Sauce:
1 medium onion, finely chopped
1 clove of garlic, crushed
1 tbsp oil
400g / 14oz canned tomatoes
1 tbsp tomato paste
½ cup water
1 sprig oregano, leaves chopped
1 tsp sugar
salt and pepper
¼ cup parsley, chopped

Place the chicken in a bowl, grate onion into the bowl, and add remaining rissole ingredients except the oil. Mix well to combine, and knead a little by hand. Roll into balls with wet hands. Heat oil in a pan and sauté the rissoles until they change color on both sides. Remove to a plate.

For the sauce, add to the pan the onion and garlic and sauté a little. Add to the pan the remaining sauce ingredients and increase the heat to boiling point. Return rissoles to the pan, reduce heat, cover and simmer for 30 minutes. Serve with spaghetti.

Chicken and Vegetable Pasta Bake

Prep and cook time: 45 minutes   Serves 4

250g / 9oz spiral pasta
30 ml / 1 fl. oz vegetable oil
500g / 18oz chicken thigh
fillets, diced
4 spring onions (scallions),
sliced
1 clove of garlic, crushed
1 courgette (zucchini), diced
150g / 5oz mushrooms, diced
¾ cup honey mustard sauce
125 ml / 4.5 fl. oz / ½ cup
cream
1½ cups fresh breadcrumbs
2 tsps parsley

Preheat the oven to 190°C (380°F). Lightly grease a large shallow casserole dish.

Cook the pasta in a saucepan of boiling water for 9–10 minutes or until tender. Drain and set aside.

Heat the oil in a large saucepan over medium heat. Add the chicken, spring onions and garlic and cook for 4 minutes.

Add the courgette, mushrooms and cream to the saucepan. Increas ethe heat to boiling point, cover and simmer for 5 minutes. Add the pasta and toss to combine. Combine the breadcrumbs with the parsley.

Spoon the pasta mixture into the large shallow casserole dish. Top with breadcrumbs and bake in the oven for 25 minutes, or until golden and crisp on top.

Note: Honey mustard sauce should be available in most grocery stores. Should you wish to make your own, heat ¼ cup red wine, ½ cup honey, 1 tsp hot English mustard, and salt and pepper to taste. Stir to combine, then allow to cool.

Chicken Livers and Mushrooms on Pasta

Prep and cook time: 1 hour 30 mins Serves: 4

500g / 18oz fresh pasta

1 tbsp olive oil

90g / 3oz Parmesan cheese, grated

Tomato Sauce:

1 tbsp vegetable oil

30g / 1oz butter

1 onion, finely diced

2 cloves of garlic, crushed

12 button mushrooms, halved

400g / 14oz canned tomatoes, mashed

1 tsp sugar

1 cup chicken stock

freshly ground black pepper

Chicken Liver Sauce:

30g / 1oz butter

250g / 9oz chicken livers, trimmed and sliced

1 sprig thyme, leaves removed

⅓ cup Marsala, or sweet white wine

¼ cup fresh parsley, chopped

To make the tomato sauce, heat oil and butter in a pan and cook onion until soft. Add garlic and mushrooms and cook for 2–3 minutes. Combine the tomatoes and sugar and add to mushrooms. Cook over a low heat for 10 minutes. Stir in the stock and simmer for 30 minutes longer or until sauce reduces and thickens. Season to taste with black pepper.

To make the chicken liver sauce, melt the butter in a saucepan and cook the chicken livers and thyme over a medium heat until brown. Increase heat, stir in Marsala and cook for 1–2 minutes, then stir in parsley.

Bring a large saucepan of salted water to the boil, add the pasta and cook until al dente. Drain and fold through the oil.

Arrange half the pasta on a warm serving platter, top with half the chicken livers, then half the tomato sauce. Sprinkle over half the Parmesan cheese, then repeat layers.

11

Chicken Spaghetti Limone

Prep and cook time: 30 minutes   Serves: 4

125 ml / 4.5 fl. oz / ½ cup
olive oil

2 cloves of garlic, crushed

1 cup fresh parsley, chopped

2 lemons, zest and juice

salt and pepper

500g / 18oz spaghetti

¾ cup pine nuts

300g / 11oz chicken, minced

Mix together half of the oil, the garlic, parsley, and lemon zest and juice. Season with salt and pepper. Stir well and set aside.

Bring a large saucepan of salted water to the boil, add the pasta and cook until just firm al dente. Just before draining, remove a small cup of pasta water. Drain the pasta and keep it warm.

Heat the remaining oil in a large pan over a medium heat and add the pine nuts, cook for 1 minute, stirring constantly. Add the chicken and fry for 4 minutes, being careful not to burn the pine nuts.

Return the pasta to the saucepan with the lemon sauce over high heat. Add a little pasta water to prevent it from drying out. Add the chicken and nuts and gently stir to combine all ingredients, remove from the heat and serve with a wedge of lemon.

Creamy Chicken and Sundried Tomato Fusilli

Prep and cook time: 25 mins

Serves: 4

500g / 18oz fusilli

300g / 11oz chicken breast, thinly sliced

300 ml / 10 fl. oz / 1¼ cups whipping cream

½ cup sundried tomato pesto

Bring a large saucepan of salted water to the boil, add the pasta and cook until al dente. Drain, set aside and keep warm.

Preheat a large non-stick frying pan on medium-high heat. Cook the chicken until browned, then remove from the pan and set aside. Reduce the heat to medium-low and add the cream and pesto. Gently simmer, stirring occasionally, for 3–4 minutes or until sauce has thickened slightly. Return the chicken to the pan and heat through.

Pour the sauce over the pasta and combine.

Duck Ragoût with Pappardelle

Prep and cook time: 40 mins   Serves: 4

750g / 1¾lb duck breasts
250g / 9oz pappardelle pasta
30 ml / 1 fl. oz olive oil
1 onion, diced
2 cloves of garlic, crushed
400g / 14oz canned tomatoes
200 ml / 7 fl. oz / ⅔ cup veal stock
salt and pepper
150g / 5oz black olives
10 fresh sage leaves

Place the duck breasts in pan, fry on both sides for 4-5 minutes and then cut the breasts into pieces and set aside.

Cook the pappardelle in salted, boiling water until al dente, and set aside.

Heat the oil, and sauté the onion and garlic for a few minutes, until onion is soft. Add the duck and sauté for 1 minute. Add the tomatoes and stock and simmer for 5–10 minutes, until the sauce thickens.

Just before serving, season with salt and pepper, add the olives and the sage leaves, and toss through the pappardelle.

14

Bacon Tagliatelle

Prep and cook time: 30 mins   Serves: 4

500g / 18oz tagliatelle
6 slices bacon
1 tsp ground cumin
¼ cup mint, chopped
3 tomatoes, diced

Bring a large saucepan of salted water to the boil, add the tagliatelle and cook until al dente. Drain, set aside and keep warm.

Place bacon on a grill and sprinkle lightly with cumin. Grill under a hot broiler for 10 minutes and then slice the bacon thinly.

Toss bacon, mint and tomatoes through cooked, hot pasta. Serve garnished with extra mint.

Variation: Replace bacon with chorizo sausage.

Gnocchi with Pork and Pepper

Prep and cook time: 1 hour 30 minutes Serves: 4

340g / 12oz pork steak, cubed

4 cloves of garlic, very finely chopped

1 tbsp dried oregano

1 lemon, juice

125ml / 4.5 fl. oz / ½ cup extra virgin olive oil

salt and black pepper

1 onion, finely chopped

3 tbsps fresh parsley, chopped

250g / 9oz yellow pepper, sliced

200ml / 7 fl oz tomato sauce

60ml / 2 fl. oz beef stock

820g / 1¾lb gnocchi

30g / 1oz black olives, pitted and sliced

Place the pork in a shallow dish and mix in half the garlic, the oregano, the lemon juice, one tablespoon of the oil and the seasoning. Cover and place in the fridge to marinate for 1 hour.

Heat the remaining oil in a large, heavy-based saucepan. Add the onion and a pinch of salt and fry for 5 minutes or until softened. Stir in the remaining garlic, parsley and pepper and cook over a low heat for 10 minutes or until the pepper begins to soften.

Mix in the tomato suce and simmer for 10 minutes, stirring often. Add the pork, its marinade and the stock. Simmer, uncovered, stirring occasionally for 10 minutes or until the sauce has thickened and the pork is cooked.

Meanwhile, cook the gnocchi in plenty of boiling, salted water until tender but still firm to the bite. Drain and transfer to a warmed bowl. Spoon over the pork sauce and toss, then scatter with the olives.

Vegetable and Prosciutto Pasta

Prep and cook time: 35 minutes   Serves: 4

1 red pepper, sliced
1 yellow pepper, sliced
1 green pepper, sliced
6 baby eggplant, thinly sliced
30ml / 1 fl.oz olive oil
250g / 9oz cherry tomatoes
8 slices of prosciutto
1 red onion, sliced
2 cloves of garlic, crushed
¼ cup basil, torn
freshly ground black pepper
500g / 18oz spinach tagliatelle

Place the red, yellow and green peppers, skin-side up, on a preheated grill and cook for 5–10 minutes until skins are blistered and charred. Place the peppers in a food bag and set aside until cool enough to handle. Remove skins from peppers.

Brush the cut surfaces of eggplant lightly with a little oil and cook on a preheated grill for 2–3 minutes each side, or until golden.

Place the tomatoes on the grill and cook for 2 minutes, or until soft.

Cook the prosciutto on a grill for 1 minute each side, or until crisp. Drain on absorbent paper and set aside.

Heat the remaining oil in a pan over a medium heat, add onion and garlic and cook, stirring, for 4 minutes or until onion is soft and golden. Add peppers, eggplant, tomatoes, basil and black pepper and cook, stirring, for 4 minutes.

Bring a large saucepan of salted water to the boil, add the pasta and cook until al dente. Drain well and top with vegetables and prosciutto.

Macaroni with Prosciutto

Prep and cook time: 40 minutes　　　Serves: 4

500g / 18oz macaroni
50g / 2oz butter
2 cloves of garlic, crushed
125g / 4½oz prosciutto, cut into strips
6 sundried tomatoes, drained and cut into strips
½ cup fresh basil, torn
freshly ground black pepper

Bring a large saucepan of salted water to the boil, add the macaroni and cook until al dente. Drain, set aside and keep warm.

Melt the butter in a large saucepan and cook garlic and prosciutto over a medium heat for 5 minutes. Add the tomatoes and basil and cook for 2 minutes longer.

Add the macaroni to pan, season to taste with black pepper, and combine.

Mushroom Bolognese

Prep and cook time: 50 minutes   Serves: 4

500g / 18oz spaghetti

Bolognese Sauce:
2 tbsps olive oil
150g / 5oz mushrooms, sliced
1 carrot, finely chopped
1 onion, finely chopped
1 clove of garlic, crushed
½ tsp chilli powder
350g / 12oz lean beef, minced
100g / 4oz prosciutto, finely chopped
ground nutmeg
¾ cup dry red wine
½ cup tomato paste
400g / 14oz canned tomatoes
½ cup water
freshly ground black pepper

To make the sauce, heat the oil in a large frying pan and cook the mushrooms, carrot and onion for 4–5 minutes, or until the onion is soft. Stir in the garlic and chilli powder and cook for 1 minute.

Add the beef and prosciutto to the pan and cook over a medium heat, stirring to break up the beef, for 4–5 minutes or until meat changes color. Drain off any fat and season to taste with nutmeg.

Stir the wine, tomato paste, tomatoes and water into pan. Increase the temperature to boiling point, then reduce heat and simmer, stirring occasionally, for 30 minutes or until sauce reduces and thickens. Season to taste with black pepper.

Bring a large saucepan of salted water to the boil, add the spaghetti and cook until al dente. Drain and place in warmed serving bowl, top with sauce and serve immediately.

Oyster Mushroom and Walnut Pasta Salad

Prep and cook time: 20 minutes   Serves: 4

500g / 18oz angel-hair pasta
½ cup olive oil
6 shallots, chopped
200g / 7oz oyster mushrooms
400g / 14oz prosciutto, sliced
2 tbsps pink or green peppercorns
2 tbsps tarragon vinegar
4 tbsps walnut oil
3 sprigs fresh tarragon
salt and freshly ground black pepper
75g / 2½oz walnuts, chopped
½ cup pine nuts, roasted

Cook pasta in plenty of boiling, salted water until tender but still firm to the bite. Drain and rinse with cold water. Pour a little oil through the pasta to prevent it sticking together. Heat the remaining olive oil in a pan and sauté the shallots, oyster mushrooms and prosciutto for 3–4 minutes.

Add peppercorns and turn off heat.

Combine the vinegar, walnut oil, tarragon, salt, pepper and walnuts, and then toss through the cooled pasta. Finally add the prosciutto, peppercorns and mushrooms, toss together and garnish with roasted pine nuts.

Pepperoni Spaghetti

Prep and cook time: 40 minutes   Serves: 4

500g / 18oz spaghetti
1 tbsp olive oil
1 onion, finely chopped
90g / 3oz black olives, chopped
125g / 4½oz pepperoni, chopped

Bring a large saucepan of salted water to the boil, add the spaghetti and cook until al dente. Drain, set aside and keep warm.

Heat the oil in a large pan and cook the onion over a medium heat for 5–6 minutes or until transparent. Add olives and pepperoni and cook for 2 minutes longer.

Add spaghetti to the pan and toss to combine.

Pork and Sage-Filled Ravioli

Prep and cook time: 30 minutes   Serves: 4

24 wonton wrappers

1 egg yolk, beaten with 1 tbsp water

40g / 2oz Parmesan cheese, grated

Pork and Sage Filling:

300g / 11oz ricotta cheese, drained

150g / 5oz lean cooked pork, diced

60g / 2oz lean bacon, finely chopped

40g / 2oz Parmesan cheese, grated

¼ cup fresh parsley, chopped

¼ cup fresh sage, chopped

ground nutmeg

freshly ground black pepper

Sage and Butter Sauce:

125g / 4½oz butter

¼ cup sage, chopped

To make the filling, place the ricotta, pork, bacon, Parmesan, parsley, sage, nutmeg and black pepper in a bowl and mix to combine.

Lay 12 wonton wrappers on bench. Place a teaspoon of the filling in the center of each one, brush the edges with egg yolk mixture and place the remaining wonton skins on top. Press the edges together.

Cook the ravioli, a few at a time, in boiling water for 4 minutes or until tender. Drain and sprinkle with Parmesan cheese.

In a saucepan, melt the butter and add the chopped sage, cook for 2 minutes. Pour over the ravioli to serve.

Calamari and Coriander Spaghetti

Prep and cook time: 25 minutes   Serves: 4

500g / 18oz calamari, cleaned, tube cut into rings

500g / 18oz spaghetti or vermicelli

2 tsps olive oil

1 red onion, finely diced

1 clove of garlic, crushed

4 tomatoes, deseeded and diced

½ cup pitted Kalamata olives, rinsed and drained, sliced

¼ cup chicken or fish stock

¼ cup dry white wine

1 cup coriander (cilantro), chopped

3 tbsps mint, chopped

freshly ground black pepper

Bring a large saucepan of water to the boil. Using a slotted spoon or wire basket, carefully lower calamari into the water. Cook for 5–10 seconds or until they just turn white and are firm. Drain. Plunge into iced water. Drain again and set aside.

Bring a large saucepan of fresh water to the boil. Add the pasta and cook until al dente.

Place the oil, onion and garlic in a non-stick skillet over a medium heat. Cook, stirring, for 3–4 minutes or until the onion is soft. Add tomatoes, olives, stock and wine. Bring to a simmer. Simmer for 5 minutes. Stir in the cilantro, mint, calamari and pepper to taste. Cook for 1–2 minutes or until heated through.

Drain the pasta. Add calamari mixture. Toss to combine.

Bucatini with Anchovy and Olive Sauce

Prep and cook time: 1 hour 15 mins   Serves: 4

500g / 18oz bucatini pasta

150g / 5oz pitted green olives, sliced

60g / 2oz Parmesan cheese, grated

60g / 2oz walnuts, finely chopped

¼ cup fresh parsley, chopped

2 sprigs fresh oregano, leaves removed and chopped

¼ cup fresh basil, chopped

2 anchovy fillets, chopped

½ cup virgin olive oil

freshly ground black pepper

Bring a large saucepan of salted water to the boil, add the pasta and cook until al dente. Drain, set aside and keep warm.

Place olives, Parmesan, walnuts, parsley, oregano, basil and anchovies in a bowl and mix to combine. Gradually mix in the oil to make a thin, smooth paste. Stand for 1 hour. Season to taste with black pepper.

Spoon sauce over pasta and serve.

Note: If the sauce is too thick, stir in 1–2 tablespoons of hot water.